In the Spotlight

Dwayne Johnson

by Kaitlyn Duling

Bullfrog Books

Ideas for Parents and Teachers

Bullfrog Books let children practice reading informational text at the earliest reading levels. Repetition, familiar words, and photo labels support early readers.

Before Reading

- Discuss the cover photo. What does it tell them?
- Look at the picture glossary together. Read and discuss the words.

Read the Book

- "Walk" through the book and look at the photos. Let the child ask questions. Point out the photo labels.
- Read the book to the child, or have him or her read independently.

After Reading

- Prompt the child to think more. Ask: What did you know about Dwayne Johnson before reading this book? What more would you like to learn about him after reading it?

Bullfrog Books are published by Jump!
5357 Penn Avenue South
Minneapolis, MN 55419
www.jumplibrary.com

Library of Congress Cataloging-in-Publication Data

Names: Duling, Kaitlyn.
Title: Dwayne Johnson / by Kaitlyn Duling.
Description: Minneapolis, Minnesota : Bullfrog Books are published by Jump!, Inc., [2018]
Series: In the spotlight | Includes index.
Identifiers: LCCN 2018010165 (print)
LCCN 2018003200 (ebook)
ISBN 9781641280365 (ebook)
ISBN 9781641280341 (hardcover : alk. paper)
ISBN 9781641280358 (pbk.)
Subjects: LCSH: Johnson, Dwayne, 1972—Juvenile literature. | Wrestlers—United States—Biography Juvenile literature. | Actors—United States Biography—Juvenile literature.
Classification: LCC GV1196.J64 (print)
LCC GV1196.J64 D85 2019 (ebook)
DDC 797.3/2092 [B]—dc23
LC record available at https://lccn.loc.gov/2018010165

Editor: Jenna Trnka
Designer: Molly Ballanger

Photo Credits: Tinseltown/Shutterstock, cover, 1; Featureflash Photo Agency/Shutterstock, 3, 4; Kathy Hutchins/Shutterstock, 5, 23tr, 24; Picture Perfect/REX/Shutterstock, 6–7; New Line/Kobal/REX/Shutterstock, 8–9, 23tl; Alberto E. Rodriguez/Getty, 10; Disney/Kobal/REX/Shutterstock, 11, 22rt; Foxvan Prods/Kobal/REX/Shutterstock, 12–13; Mark Schiefelbein/AP Images, 14; Michael Loccisano/Getty, 15; Rodrigo Varela/Getty, 16–17, 23bl; Jon Furniss/Getty, 18–19; Andreas Rentz/Getty, 20–21, 23br; Moviestore Collection/REX/Shutterstock, 22l; Willy Sanjuan/Invision/AP/REX/Shutterstock, 22br.

Printed in the United States of America at Corporate Graphics in North Mankato, Minnesota.

Table of Contents

The Rock 4

Key Events 22

Picture Glossary 23

Index 24

To Learn More 24

The Rock

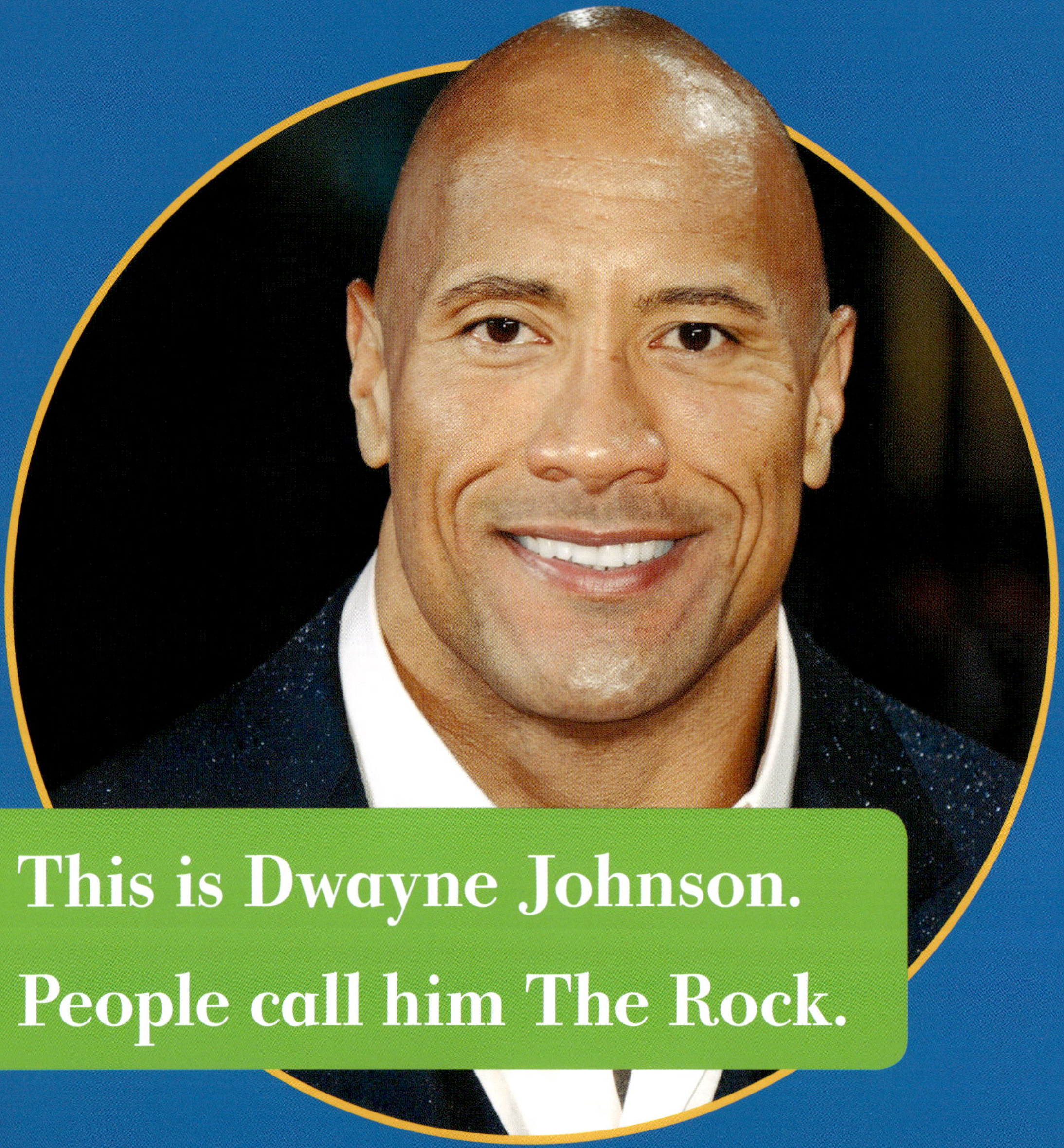

This is Dwayne Johnson.
People call him The Rock.

He is famous.

Why?

He was a wrestler.

The Rock was his name.

Now he is an actor.

He is in movies.

Moana is one.

He is the voice of Maui.

Dwayne is funny.

He likes to make people laugh.

Dwayne sings.

He dances, too!

Dwayne donates.
He gives money.
He helps.

2006
Date September 8th
oundation $ 170,000
nd Dollars 00/100
Dollars

DWAYNE "THE ROCK" JOHNSON
THE GAME PLAN

He visits kids who are sick.

Fans like Dwayne.

And he likes them!

fans

Key Events

May 2, 1972:
Dwayne Douglas Johnson is born in Hayward, California.

November 17, 1996:
Dwayne has his first wrestling match on TV.

May 4, 2001:
The Mummy Returns, Dwayne's first feature film, premieres.

October 2, 2007:
Dwayne donates $1 million to the University of Miami, where he went to college.

November 23, 2016:
Moana premieres.
Dwayne is the voice of Maui.

December 13, 2017:
Dwayne receives a star on the Hollywood Walk of Fame.

Picture Glossary

actor
Someone who performs in a play, TV show, or movie.

famous
Very well-known to many people.

donates
Gives something, such as money, to a charity.

fans
People who are very interested in and enthusiastic about something or someone.

Index

actor 8
dances 15
donates 16
funny 13
helps 16
kids 19
laugh 13
Maui 11
Moana 10
movies 8
sings 14
wrestler 7

To Learn More

Learning more is as easy as 1, 2, 3.

1) Go to www.factsurfer.com

2) Enter "DwayneJohnson" into the search box.

3) Click the "Surf" button to see a list of websites.

With factsurfer.com, finding more information is just a click away.